M000191700

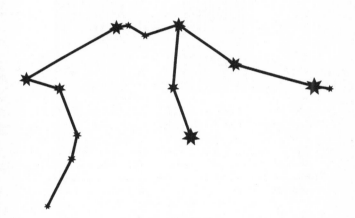

ONE IDEA PRESS

Ordering Information:
Quantity sales. Special discounts are available on quantity purchases by
corporations, associations, and others. For details, contact the "Special Sales
Department" at the following email address: hello@oneideapress.com.

Paperback Edition: 978-1-944134-50-1
Hardback Edition: 978-1-944134-51-8

Printed in the United States of America

Aquarius

a love letter

Heidi Rose Robbins

with illustrations by
Wyoh Lee

hello love.

(yes, you)

Friends,

I'm so glad you are holding this book! It is filled with encouragement and an ongoing invitation for us all to be more fully who we are.

The best way to work with these books is to purchase one for each of your signs — your Sun, Moon, and Rising Sign.

These are the three most important positions in your astrological chart. You can discover what these are if you enter your exact time, date, and place of birth in any online astrology site. Each position has something unique to offer.

When you read the book for your Moon, think of it as an energy that is very available to you. It's a place where you might feel comfortable. The Moon has to do with our emotional life, our patterns of behavior, and circumstances of our childhood. We can rely on the Moon, but we also want to work to shed the patterns that no longer serve us.

The Sun is our present personality. We can learn a lot about our everyday self in the world. We can learn about the energies we have readily available to us to use in service to our highest calling.

The Rising Sign is the most important point. It is the sign that was rising as we took our first breath. It holds the key to our soul's calling. It is an energy we want to cultivate and be generous with throughout our lives.

So — enjoy the journey. Be sure to read them all!

My dear Aquarius,

This little book is a love letter to your innovative and freedom loving self. It is written to remind you of your many gifts. It is written to be a loving mirror so any page can remind you who you truly are. Take it in, dear Aquarius. Breathe in the original, improvisational being that is YOU. See your experimental, color-outside-the-lines self in these pages.

This little book will also explore those places in ourselves that start to close when we want to open, the part of us that hesitates when we want to act. We all have our quirks and difficulties, after all. But if we return again and again to our potency, vulnerability and sense of possibility, we can outgrow our closures one by one.

Think of this book as a treasure chest containing the golden coins of YOU. Open it when you wish to remember your beauty, worth or great potential. And remember, too, this Aquarius part of you is just one voice in the symphony of YOU. It cannot possibly contain your complexity and bounty. But it can begin to name just a few of your gifts.

Read this out loud when you can. Read this in the morning. Read it before bed. Read it when you need encouragement. Read it even if you are already feeling full of brilliant, unique ideas. Let it fuel you. Own it and use it and claim it! This is your love letter, Aquarius. This is the song of YOU.

Big love,
Heidi Rose

Celebrating Aquarius

As you read this celebration, you will sometimes say "Yes, yes, yes! This is me!" And you may likewise sometimes feel that you have not yet lived into some of these qualities. This is honoring and celebrating the very best of your Aquarius energy. This is naming the full, conscious, awakened use of your Aquarius gifts. We are sounding the note of THE POSSIBLE. So, even if you feel you still have work to do in certain areas — as do we all — let these words be inspiration to offer your best Self!

You relish your
independence.

You are best without a boss. You
like to call your own shots. Even
in relationships, you need lots of
solo time. You think and act for
yourself. You are a free agent.

You are undeniably yourself, one of a kind, totally original, a rare bird.

You are unique, dear Aquarius. You go your own way. You don't apologize for being exactly who you are. You don't need to explain yourself. Your authenticity and originality inspire others to claim their own rare bird self.

You color outside
the lines and follow
your own uncharted path.

You have always been a free
agent, forging your own path.
You do not go the way of others,
nor do you often follow the
suggestions of how something
might be done. You are a solo and
experimental flyer.

You share your resources.

You love to share. You love to
distribute what is available
to the entire group. You will often
wait to take your share until
everyone else has been served.
You love to barter and
exchange as well.

You empower and uplift the group.

You love team work. You love to be a part of something. Your presence in any group strengthens the group because you will always stand for the benefit of all. You tend to quietly hold the group or subtly facilitate the group instead of leading outright.

You solve problems.

You assess the situation, dear Aquarius. You look at the problem from many different angles. You don't get emotionally involved. You keep your eye on the prize and bring a great curiosity to each problem. If something doesn't work, you simply experiment and try again.

You always offer a unique perspective.

You love a good bird's eye view. You rise above whatever is unfolding and look at it from another angle. You always address the things others are not noticing. You bring the new thought into the room.

You improvise and innovate.

You are good at winging it. You are willing to dive in without much planning or study. You like to try out what is new. You like to push the boundaries of the known. You love the exciting territory when you've stepped off the beaten path.

You are a natural server.

You don't like to call much attention to yourself. You'd rather serve the moment and the movement. You play your part. You participate with the group momentum. You like to remain anonymous.

You can detach from
overly emotional situations
and offer wisdom.

One of your super powers is
your ability to not take things
personally. You work in the mental
realm to solve the problems that
arise. You do not spend much
time in the realm of emotional
struggle. This gives you a unique
perspective.

You believe in democracy
and equality.

Freedom for all. Everyone gets
a vote. No one is better than
any other. We are all part of one
great experiment. You stand for
the collective and individual
voices of the people, dear
Aquarius. You know that we
are strongest when ALL are
equally heard.

You are a humanitarian.

You see Humanity as a whole and want the best for us. You want to help those that have been ignored or left behind. You promote our collective welfare and want to address the big issues that are crippling our health and joy.

You love to share good information. You give freely.

You like to distribute and circulate information that benefits the collective. You are the 'water-bearer' after all, and you like to pour forth nourishment for those that need it most. Nourishment often comes in the form of information that we need to take care of ourselves and progress.

You love universally.

You love impersonally and wholly.
You are often less interested in
the idea of an intense personal
love and more interested in
how we all can learn to love one
another as fellow human beings.

You live for freedom and
cannot be contained.

You will not be held in check. You
love to know that nothing and
no one pins you down. You love no
strings attached. You believe
everyone has a right to this kind
of expansive freedom.

You love inspiring
collaboration.

You deeply believe in and invest
in the group or the team. You
love to hear from everybody.
It's important to you that all
participate, that all offer their
vision or their viewpoint. You want
whatever is created to have
come from the entire group.

You embrace and explore
cutting-edge technology.

You always look to the future.
What is happening right NOW?
What is currently being invented,
created, developed? You want to
know and you want to participate.
You are always looking forward.

You want to change the world.

You certainly believe we can build a better world and you want to be a part of it. You care about the future and well-being of Humanity and you know there are many places we need to wake up and fast. You want to help that great awakening.

You don't take it personally.

You have a great ability to detach from personal attack. You refuse to let the personal into debate. You want to talk about what matters and you simply ignore the personal affronts.

You are willing to sacrifice
the needs of the personal
for the greater good.

You are often willing to give up
your own personal needs for the
needs of the group at large. You
will support whatever benefits
the most people even if it means
sacrificing your own preferences
or comforts.

You are a good friend.

You love to extend your hand in
friendship. You look to create soul-
friendships. And you are a friend
to your fellow human, the trees,
the rushing river, the animals.
You offer your presence, clarity,
and love.

Living Your Aquarius Love

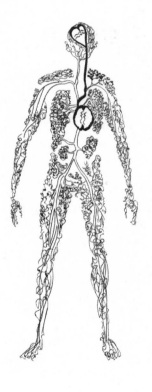

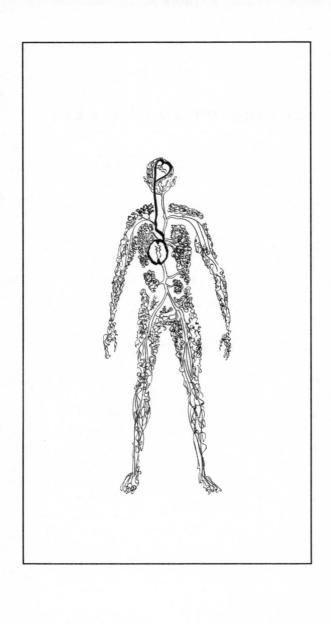

How are you feeling, dear Aquarius? Can you sense the potency of your gifts? Do you want to make the very most of this innovative, cutting-edge energy of Aquarius? Here are some thoughts about how to live fully into your Aquarius love and how to nourish your Aquarius spirit. Consider them little whispered reminders meant to help you THRIVE. Consider them 'action items' — a loving Aquarius "to-do" list. Consider them invitations to live your fullest maverick, freedom-loving life.

Find the people with whom you feel the deepest connection in service and creativity and then go out and do good in the world.

This could be a creative ensemble or a group that has gathered to improve conditions. Call in the allies that want to get to work! Remember President Lincoln's 'Team of Rivals.' He invited many who disagreed with him into his inner circle to make sure his constituents were fully represented. He didn't take their disagreement personally.

Choose Your Cause
and Dive in.

Choose a cause and get
tenacious. Bring your problem
solving, innovative eye and get to
work. If it feels like a huge task,
keep inviting others to join to the
work. Create engagement.

Think with your heart and love with your mind.

Always try to strike a balance and a working relationship between your heart and mind. The heart has an intelligence and the mind must be infused with compassion. When this relationship is at work, we cannot help but address all issues with consciousness and grace.

Offer your objective perspective.

Your objectivity will always be
refreshing. We lose so much time
and precious energy wrestling
in our personal dramas with one
another. Your Aquarian spirit
knows how to detach and sound
a higher note. You bring clarity.

Call your allies.

There are always those who
will understand and want to help
you if you intention is pure and
your mission is for the good.
Call all those who will play a role
in your Aquarian team. They
are waiting.

Pour forth your love wisdom.

You are the water-bearer.
You are actually here on this
planet to be a distributor of
love and wisdom. You can
quench Humanity's thirst with
your offerings.

Gather and strengthen
on-line communities or improve
the way we connect on-line.

You always will have new ideas
about how we might gather and
connect. And because you are
often tapped into cutting-edge
technology, you can help create
more and more intimacy in how
we meet on-line. Do your best to
help infuse technology with love.

Barter, distribute, Share.

Always offer alternative ways
of working with resources. Our
current financial structures
are changing. Be in on the
revolutionary ways we can work
with money. Help create a culture
where we share, exchange and
trade more.

Growing Your Aquarius Love

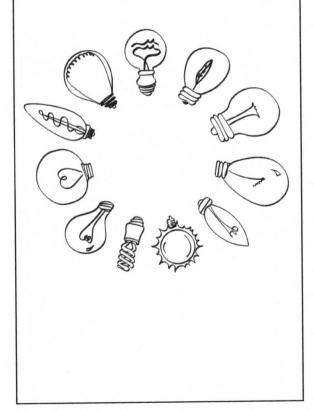

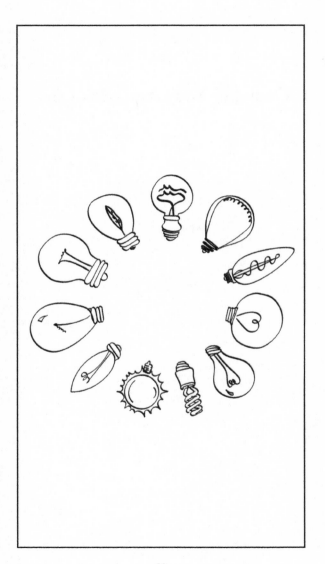

Sometimes, dear Aquarius, we swing too far in one direction and need to invite a balancing energy to set us right. We are all growing and need to address the parts of ourselves that have not developed as fully. The opportunity for Aquarius is to invite Leo (your opposite sign) into the picture. Here are ways to grow your Aquarius love to be more personal, expressive and spontaneous.

Do not remain aloof.

It's too easy to detach, dear Aquarius. And sometimes it's easy to feel a bit proud of your own detachment. You might wonder why others can't be as clear, objective and detached as you. However, sometimes it's necessary to get right into the thick of the conversation, as messy as it may be. No one has it all figured out. Don't remove yourself from the sometimes more emotional exchange.

Refuse to be the "lone wolf."

It's easy to feel misunderstood, or that no one really gets what you are trying to do. Don't fall prey to that belief. There are allies everywhere. No matter how brilliant and original we each are, there are others who share and are working on similar ideas. Find them! Don't isolate.

Don't be a rebel
just to be a rebel.

Sometimes we just say 'no' to
make a statement. "No one will
ever tell me what to do or how
to do it." If there is something
that demands revolution, then
act. But don't rebel against
everything and everyone. It gets
very lonely.

It's okay to SHINE now and then.

You are definitely a lover of the group. And you will often encourage everyone in the group to have their say. Sometimes, though, a group needs YOUR specific guidance. Come forth and shine.

Practice talking about your emotional life.

Though you tend to be more mentally polarized, it's good to practice sharing how you FEEL now and then. Your loved ones will be grateful. Offer your love in new ways — ways that might even make you a little uncomfortable. This is your edge.

Don't lose yourself
in the group.

Sometimes Aquarius is called
"The Gregarious Aquarius." This
is the opposite of the lone wolf. It
just wants to lose itself in a group
ideal or group rebellion. Make
sure you are thinking for yourself
within the context of the group.
All groups are not conscious groups.

Check any arrogance.

You are smart, smart, smart. You are even BRILLIANT. But don't let that create separation. Lean into love for your fellow human. Recognize each person's unique offering. Recognize the many different forms of intelligence!

Questions to Inspire
Sharing Your Aquarius Love

Dear Aquarius, here are a few questions and prompts that might inspire or clarify your mission. Grab your journal. Write for 15 minutes about each. Address one every day for awhile. Read your answers out loud to a friend. Let this exploration spark your next great group work.

Who is on my team?

I feel most free when I...

Here are some of my
spiritual brothers
and sisters...
I consider them so
because...

What do I have to say
to my community?

We are not alone.

What is one problem I'd like to address on our planet and who are the members of my dream team to go about addressing it?

If you really knew me,
you'd know...

Yes we can...
(Keep returning to this
phrase...)

One Last Little Love Note:

Aquarius, I hope those questions spark many new brainstorms, experiments and community efforts in your life. You have so much to offer, so much to give. Your innovation and authenticity inspire so many. If you ever need encouragement, just dip into this little book for a reminder of your light.

Now go forth Aquarius, and do your thing.

The World is Waiting for YOU.

Big love,
Heidi Rose

About the Author.

Heidi grew up with an astrologer father and an architect mother. Her father taught her the zodiac with her ABC's and her mother taught her to love art and appreciate the beauty of the natural world. She likes to call herself a poet with a map of the heavens in her pocket. Her passion is to inspire and encourage us all to be our truest, most authentic, radiant selves using the tools of astrology and poetry.

www.heidirose.com
Instagram @heidiroserobbins

Made in the USA
Monee, IL
21 November 2021